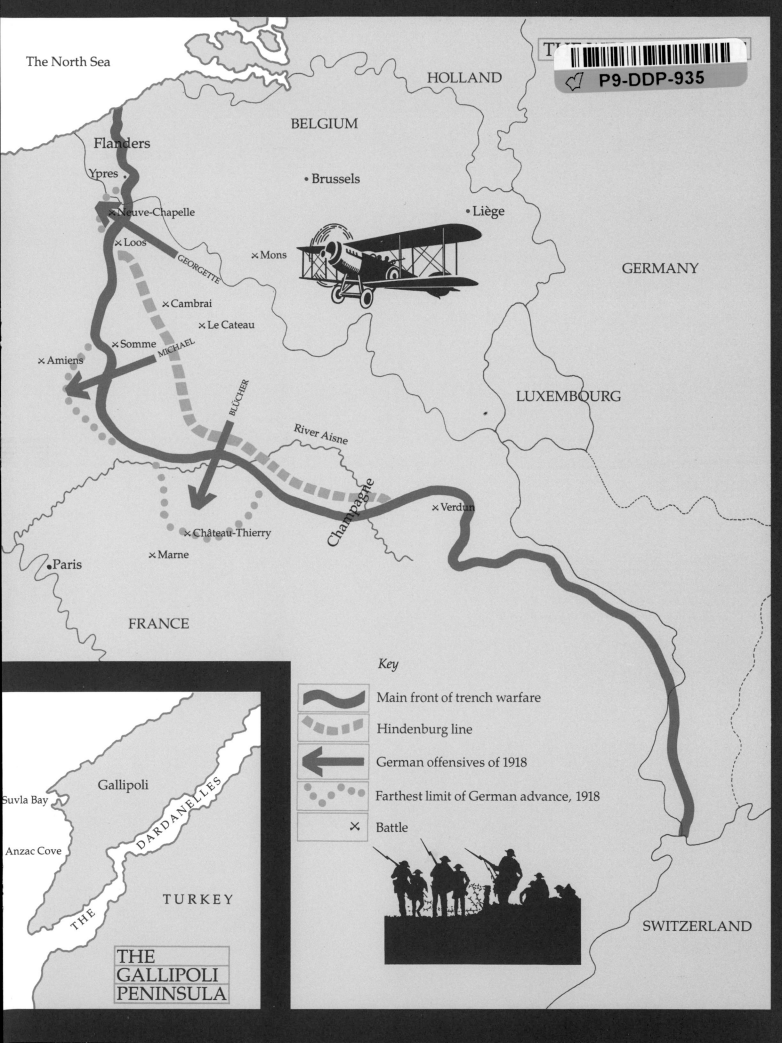

The North Sea

HOLLAND

BELGIUM

Flanders

Ypres

×Neuve-Chapelle

×Loos   GEORGETTE

×Cambrai

×Le Cateau

×Somme   MICHAEL

×Amiens

•Brussels

•Liège

GERMANY

×Mons

LUXEMBOURG

BLÜCHER

River Aisne

Champagne

×Verdun

×Château-Thierry

×Marne

•Paris

FRANCE

Key

Main front of trench warfare

Hindenburg line

German offensives of 1918

Farthest limit of German advance, 1918

× Battle

Suvla Bay

Gallipoli

Anzac Cove

THE DARDANELLES

THE

TURKEY

THE
GALLIPOLI
PENINSULA

SWITZERLAND

FIRST
WORLD WAR

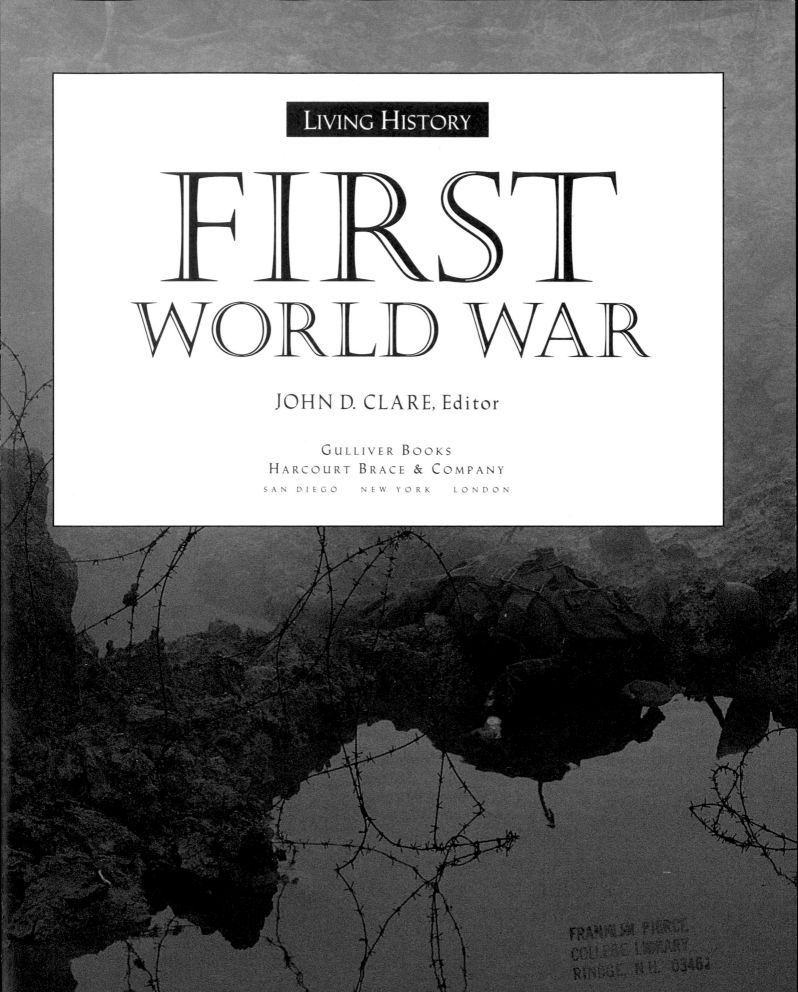

LIVING HISTORY

FIRST WORLD WAR

JOHN D. CLARE, Editor

GULLIVER BOOKS
HARCOURT BRACE & COMPANY
SAN DIEGO   NEW YORK   LONDON

HARCOURT
BRACE

First published in Great Britain in 1994 by Riverswift,
Random House

Library of Congress Cataloging-in-Publication Data
First World War/John D. Clare, editor. — 1st U.S. ed.
    p.   cm. — (Living history)
"Gulliver Books."
"First published in Great Britain in 1994 by Riverswift,
Random House" — T.p. verso.
Includes bibliographical references.
ISBN 0-15-200087-9
1. World War, 1914–1918 — Juvenile literature. [1. World War,
1914–1918.] I. Clare, John D., 1952–   . II. Series: Living history
(San Diego, Calif.)
D522.7.F55   1995
940.3 — dc20   94-7875

Director of Photography   Tymn Lintell
Photography   Charles Best
Art Director   Dalia Hartman
Production Manager, Photography   Fiona Nicholson
Typesetting   Thompson Type, San Diego, California
Reproduction   Scantrans, Singapore

ACKNOWLEDGMENTS

Historical Advisor: Laurie Miller, Imperial War Museum, London. **Cast-
ing:** Baba's Crew; Carol Lee; Barbara Stammers. **Illustrations:** David
Wire (map and timeline), Antony Parks (pp. 32–33). **Jacket Concept:**
Peter Bennett. **Makeup:** Jane Jamieson. **Maps and Timeline:** John Laing.
Model Aircraft: David Bodington. **Set Building:** Upset. **Special Effects:**
Mark Holt. **Transport and Construction:** Peter Knight, Road Runner
Film Services.

Additional photographs: Bettmann Archive, N.Y., pp. 48–49. Bibliothek
Für Zeitgeschichte, pp. 12–13. Bridgeman Art Library/Wyllie Gallery,
p. 7. Brooke Bond Foods Ltd., p. 56 (top). L (Néry) Battery, 1st Regiment
Royal Horse Artillery, Hants: Fortuno Mantania, pp. 16–17. Militaria
Magazine/Histoire & Collections, Paris, p. 16. Hulton Deutsch, p. 7
(top); p. 15; pp. 18–19; pp. 30–31. Imperial War Museum, p. 23; p. 28;
pp. 28–29; pp. 32–33; p. 32; p. 33 (top left); p. 33 (bottom right); pp. 38–
39; p. 42; pp. 44–45; p. 45 (top); pp. 50–51; p. 55; p. 56 (bottom left);
pp. 58–59; p. 59; p. 62 (top right). David King Collection, pp. 36–37.
National Archives, Washington D.C., pp. 46–47, p. 49, p. 62 (left). National Maritime Museum, p. 47. Peter Newark, p. 55 (top), p. 56 (bottom
right), p. 61 (top). Novosti, London, p. 37. Tony Stone/Michael Busselle,
pp. 42–43 (background). Süddeutscher Verlag, p. 6, p. 63 (top). Ullstein
Bilderdienst, pp. 10–11, p. 46. Weimar Archive, Shrops., p. 25. Heloise
Wire/Historial de la Grande Guerre, cover bottom left, p. 27, p. 29, p. 63
(bottom).

Contents

Toward Disaster

The First World War, which lasted from 1914 to 1918, was known at the time as the Great War. It involved more countries than any previous war; it introduced new technology into fighting; and it caused destruction on an unequaled scale. It was "total war," involving the mobilization not just of vast armies but of whole nations.

More than 65 million men fought in the First World War; over 8 million of them were killed. In addition, nearly 9 million civilians died — from starvation, disease, artillery fire, and air raids. In France and Belgium, where most of the fighting occurred, the war destroyed 300,000 houses, 6,000 factories, 1,000 miles (1,600 kilometers) of rail lines, and 112 coal mines. Even for those who survived, the cost of the war was devastating.

When the war finally ended, it was only natural for people to ask, "Why did this happen?" On June 28, 1919, seven months after the end of hostilities, the victorious nations met to sign the Treaty of Versailles; they blamed Germany for starting the conflict. In Article 231 of the treaty, Germany was said to be responsible for "all the loss and damage to which the Allied Governments . . . have been subjected." The defeated Germans had no choice but to sign the treaty, though Article 231 galled them. During the 1920s, a special branch of the German Foreign Office — the War Guilt Section — published all Germany's official war documents to try to prove it had not caused the war. After studying these papers, some historians (called revisionists) agreed. One of them, an American historian named Sidney Bradshaw Fay, suggested instead that certain general factors had worked together to create a tense situation in Europe; he claimed war had been bound to break out sooner or later.

According to Sidney Bradshaw Fay, nationalism, or an extreme sense of loyalty to one's own nation, created much of the tension in pre-war Europe. "Rule Britannia," an anthem praising British naval strength, was heard everywhere in Great Britain. Italy and Germany were each proud to have achieved unification (Italy in 1861 and Germany in 1871) after having spent centuries divided into many smaller states. The Germans adopted "Deutschland Über Alles" ("Germany Over All") as their national anthem, and many Germans predicted that Germany, with its growing industrial strength, would soon gain a new position of power in the world.

In eastern Europe, particularly in the Balkans, nationalism threatened the power of two old empires. The Turkish empire was losing territory to groups including Bulgarian, Greek, and Serb nationalists who sought to end Turkish control of their lands. Austria-Hungary, which bordered the Balkans to the north and west, also felt threatened by the growing nationalism there; in particular it feared the aggressive

Serb nationalists who were intent on expanding their domain.

Adding to the tension in Europe was a complex system of treaties and alliances. The major states of Europe had formed themselves into two opposing alliances that, in theory, were equally balanced. In 1882, Germany and Austria-Hungary (together known as the Central Powers) formed the Triple Alliance with Italy. By 1907, France, Russia, and Great Britain made a less formal pact called the Triple Entente. European leaders believed that this system of alliances would create a "balance of power" that would prevent war from breaking out — but as frequent international crises

showed, the balance they had created was fragile.

A growing militarism across Europe added to the danger of war. By 1914, Germany had trained 8.5 million soldiers who could be called up for the army, Russia nearly 4.5 million, France over 3.5 million, and Austria-Hungary 3 million. Britain lacked a large peacetime army, but its navy was almost equal to all the other European navies put together. When their supremacy at sea was threatened by a German naval building program in 1898, the British responded with a building program of their own, and a naval arms race began.

European imperialism also contributed to tension. Throughout the 19th century, Europeans had sought to gain control of

foreign countries and their markets, and by 1914, most of the rest of the world — with the exception of the United States and the countries of Central and South America — was under the political and economic domination of Europe's industrialized nations. The British controlled India and dreamed of an empire in Africa stretching from Cairo to Cape Town. The French, who wanted to establish a north African empire, also had their eyes on Cairo. Germany was a relatively new imperial power, and its empire was small (comprising only some parts of Africa and a few tiny colonies in the Pacific), but the Germans were eager to add to their territory, even if this meant challenging other European powers.

In 1911, a crisis arose when a German gunboat called the *Panther* sailed into Agadir in Morocco; the move provoked France, which claimed special rights in Morocco. Britain supported France and put its own huge navy on a war footing. Faced with Anglo-French cooperation, Germany backed down. War was avoided, but the tension between the European powers was revealed. As one of American president Woodrow Wilson's advisers told him: "It only needs a spark to set the whole thing off."

Far left: *Many of Europe's rulers are related. The family of Queen Victoria of Great Britain (seated, center) includes Kaiser Wilhelm of Germany (seated, left) and Czar Nicholas of Russia (standing next to him).*
Above left: *To compete with the growing German navy, Britain builds eight large warships called dreadnoughts.*
Above: *The German army signs up recruits in Togoland.*

Murder at Sarajevo

In 1914, a small Austrian province called Bosnia provided the setting for the touchy European situation to explode. Bosnia bordered the Serbian state, which had won its independence from the Turks in the 1840s and was still aggressively seeking territory. Because Bosnia had a large population of ethnic Serbs, many Austrians feared that Serbia would attack Austria and try to annex Bosnia. The Austrians felt their neighbors needed to be taught a lesson — especially once the world learned of the Black Hand, an organization formed in 1911 to win Serbian unity through acts of terrorism. Between January 1913 and June 1914, the Austrian army chief of staff recommended going to war with Serbia on 25 occasions. In the summer of 1914, as a show of strength, Austria sent 70,000 troops on maneuvers to Bosnia.

On June 28, 1914, Archduke Franz Ferdinand, heir to the throne of Austria-Hungary, went to the Bosnian capital of Sarajevo to review the Austrian troops stationed there; his wife, Sophie, accompanied him. Austrian spies in Serbia had warned of a possible assassination attempt, but the trip went forward nonetheless. As their motorcade made its way down Sarajevo's main street, 120 policemen guarded the route — and six young Serbian men, holding guns and bombs supplied by the Black Hand, waited to try to kill the archduke.

Franz Ferdinand's car passed two conspirators without incident. But then the car passed the third conspirator, Cabrinovič, who threw a bomb. The bomb bounced off the back of the archduke's car and blew up the car behind. Alerted to danger, the motorcade sped away to the town hall. The conspirators seemed to have missed their chance.

At the town hall, the archduke decided to cancel his visit and return by a different route. Confused about the new plan, the archduke's driver made a wrong turn onto a narrow side road. General Potiorek, the governor of Bosnia, who was riding in the car with the royal couple, shouted to the driver to reverse. But as the archduke's car backed up slowly, a fourth conspirator, Gavrilo Princip, appeared, drew his revolver, and fired. The first shot hit Franz Ferdinand in the neck. A second, aimed at Potiorek, hit Sophie in the stomach. Within moments, Franz Ferdinand and Sophie were dead.

The Serbian terrorists had achieved their goal, but the consequences of the murders would reach far beyond Bosnia, Serbia, and Austria-Hungary. "If I had forseen what was to happen," said Cabrinovič later, "I should have sat down on the bombs and blown myself to bits."

Across Europe the assassination of Archduke Franz Ferdinand is front-page news, but few people realize that it will lead to a world war.

The Sooner the Better

Franz Ferdinand's murder outraged Kaiser Wilhelm of Germany. He was eager to see Germany assume its "place in the sun," and he feared that the assassination would weaken Germany's ally Austria-Hungary and might even bring that empire to the verge of collapse. "Now or never. . . . It is high time a clean sweep was made of the Serbs," he wrote on June 30, 1914. Kaiser Wilhelm found support among the German army commanders. "We are ready, and the sooner the better for us," said General Helmuth von Moltke, who claimed that war offered "the last means of preserving Austria-Hungary."

On July 5, therefore, Wilhelm assured the Austrian government that it could "in this case, as in all others, rely on Germany's full support." The next day, he referred to the Agadir crisis of 1911 when he told a friend, "This time I won't chicken out."

On July 23, the Austrian government sent the Serbian government a forcefully worded ten-point ultimatum requiring it to stamp out all opposition to Austria-Hungary. Point Six demanded an inquiry into Franz Ferdinand's assassination, at which Austrian delegates were to be present and active. The Austrian government intended that the terms of this ultimatum would be impossible to accept. Because Serbia would lose its rights of government if it agreed to all of Austria's demands, the Serbs would surely reject the ultimatum; in this way, Austria would appear justified in declaring war. To make any diplomatic solution to the crisis more difficult, Serbia was given a mere 48 hours to reply.

Russia, alarmed at the growth of Austrian power in the Balkans, sent the Serbs a strong letter of support. Despite this offer,

the Serbian government tried to avoid a conflict. They responded quickly and accepted all the Austrian demands except Point Six, which went against Serbian law.

The Austrian government, however, was not interested in compromise; on July 28, 1914, it sent a telegram to Serbia, declaring war. Later that day, Austrian guns began to bombard the Serbian capital, Belgrade.

For two days, the Russian government debated how to respond. Few Russians wanted war. Russia, however, had promised to support the Serbs; to let the Austrians destroy Serbia would damage Russia's prestige. Czar Nicholas was at first uncertain what to do, but on July 31, determined to act decisively, he ordered his army commanders to prepare for action and mobilize the troops.

The Russian decision to mobilize quickly escalates the conflict. When the German chancellor, Theobald von Bethmann-Hollweg, asks General Moltke, "Is the Fatherland in danger?" the reply is, "Yes!"

In response, the German army also prepares for action. German reservists are called up for military service. Boarding trains and waving to their wives and sweethearts, they are eager to go to war; like the kaiser, they don't want Germany to back down this time.
Left: A German cartoon shows Germany and Austria facing many enemies. Only their military strength, represented by the shell, keeps the balance of power (and even gives them a bit of an advantage). In the middle, Turkey, America, and Italy are not yet committed to either side.

Sliding into War

After years of building up their armed forces, each nation except Britain had millions of reservists awaiting the summons to war. The quickest way of transporting these large numbers of men was by rail, and the plans for doing so were immensely complicated. Each army, therefore, had only one or two plans for mobilization, and it *had* to follow those plans exactly.

Russia's Plan A involved moving troops into position for an attack on eastern Germany. The German plan, devised between 1897 and 1905 by the army chief of staff, Alfred von Schlieffen, was based on the assumption that if Germany went to war, it would be against both France and Russia. German army strategists were not really worried about France; in 1870, the German army had defeated the French in less than ten weeks. They were much more afraid of the huge Russian army, but most people

thought that it would take the Russians weeks to mobilize their men. The Schlieffen plan anticipated a French attack on Alsace-Lorraine; it put the strongest units of the German army to the north. When the French attacked, these units would sweep through Belgium and circle behind the French, quickly destroying them. The German army could then be transported by train to the Eastern Front in time to confront the invading Russians.

Even as Russia and Germany began to follow their plans and mobilize their vast forces in the late summer of 1914, nobody wanted or expected war. They thought that, as during the Agadir crisis in 1911, someone would back down and war would be avoided, but events developed a momentum of their own. Germany declared war on Russia on August 1, 1914. The same day, the British foreign secretary, Sir Edward Grey, told the German government that Britain would remain neutral if Germany did not attack France. Kaiser Wilhelm was

delighted: "This calls for champagne; we must halt the march to the west." Eleven thousand trains, however, were on the move in Germany, carrying the soldiers to the Western Front. The German army was due to invade Belgium in three days' time. Moltke told the kaiser, "It is impossible, the whole army would be thrown into confusion." Kaiser Wilhelm was no longer in control of events; the mobilization continued.

On August 2, the German army asked permission to pass through Belgium. The Belgian government refused; nonetheless 1.5 million German soldiers crossed the border. On August 3, claiming that French airplanes had bombed a German town, Germany declared war on France.

On August 4, Britain sent an ultimatum demanding, by midnight, a German promise to withdraw from Belgium. A treaty dating from 1839 obliged Britain to defend Belgium in the event of an invasion, but still the Germans were amazed by the demand. Most Britons, however, agreed with Sir Edward Grey that the prospect of German domination of Europe was "disagreeable." That night, crowds gathered in Parliament Square in London. As the clock struck 11 P.M. (midnight in Berlin), they sang "God Save the King" and then ran home, "crying aloud rather hysterically, 'War! War! War!'" As Grey watched the crowds disperse, he commented, "The lights are going out all over Europe: we shall not see them lit again in our lifetime."

Meanwhile, most of the 120,000 Americans stranded in Europe were trying desperately to return home. In the United States, former president Theodore Roosevelt wrote soon after the outbreak that both sides of the conflict were equally justified. He noted that America was "well-nigh alone among the great civilized powers in being unshaken by the present world-wide war," and that "for this we should be humbly and profoundly grateful."

In 1914, German ammunition limbers (left) and German soldiers (below) are on the move. The soldiers' distinctive helmets are made of leather with a brass spike; these helmets do not give much protection against bullets.

Joining Up

As more and more countries were drawn into the developing conflict, army reservists all over mainland Europe enthusiastically boarded trains to go to war. In Russia, they left joyously, dancing to the music of the balalaika. For many, war seemed preferable to the diplomatic tensions and crises of the last few years. "Gone was the pressure, gone was the uncertainty. . . . And then I was struck by a fierce hatred for those who had disturbed the peace," wrote the German artist Ludwig Thoma.

In Britain, the government launched a massive recruiting campaign featuring posters of Lord Kitchener, the British secretary of war, fiercely pointing his finger at the onlooker and saying: "Your Country Needs YOU."

The campaign was a tremendous success and there were not enough recruiting stations to cope with the flood of volunteers who rushed to enlist, fearing the war would be over by Christmas and determined "by hook or by crook not to miss it." "Isn't it just luck to have been born just the right age and in just the right place," wrote the English poet Julian Grenfell. Across the British Empire, men signed up in Australia, Canada, New Zealand, India, even Egypt. Sixty thousand Americans — frustrated by their own country's neutrality and responding to British propaganda representing the Germans as Huns, and the French and English as the champions of Western civilization — wrote to the Canadian Militia Department, offering to join the Canadian Expeditionary Force.

Patriotism lay behind much of the initial enthusiasm for the war. Fear and hatred of the enemy were also common. British newspapers claimed that "Huns" had roasted Belgian children over fires and trampled babies underfoot. In Germany, many people believed the Russians to be capable of any atrocity: "It was Germany fighting for her life, the German nation for its . . . freedom and its future. [It was] the greatest and most unforgettable period of my life," a German corporal named Adolf Hitler remembered later.

In addition, many welcomed war for its own sake. The Swedish writer Sven Hedin joined the German army simply "because I wanted . . . to become familiar with war as it really is." War was thought to be noble and purifying. "I've been waiting for it these last 40 years. . . . France is pulling herself together and it's my opinion she couldn't have done that without being purged by war," wrote a French clergyman in August 1914. To the German novelist Ernst Glaeser it seemed that war had "made the world beautiful."

Training is routine and repetitive, designed to make the men obey without question. Here French recruits learn to use the bayonet. Although the generals on both sides place great trust in the bayonets' "cold steel," German soldiers find that their entrenching spades make better weapons in hand-to-hand fighting.
Below: *The Canadian Cyclist Corps riding in Britain in 1915. Troops come from a number of German colonies and from all parts of the British and French empires, only to die far from home on the battlefields of western Europe.*

First Moves

In the first weeks of August 1914, the German army swept across Belgium. It took Liège on August 7 and Brussels 13 days later, driving back the French army, which had advanced to meet it. On August 21, the British Expeditionary Force (BEF), which comprised only 125,000 men, arrived to join the French. It was rumored that the kaiser had sneered at what he called a "contemptible little army." Twice, however — at Mons (August 23) and Le Cateau (August 26) — the British held up the Germans, allowing the French to retreat in good order.

In Alsace-Lorraine, the French mounted an attack but failed to overcome the Germans. Dressed in old-fashioned blue coats and bright red trousers, their cavalry wearing breastplates and helmets, the French soldiers advanced heroically, only to be massacred by German artillery and machine-gun fire. Officers, whom the Germans immediately identified by the white gloves they wore, suffered especially. Fearing the advancing German troops, the French government fled from Paris to Bordeaux; in Berlin, the kaiser thought the war had already been won.

By the beginning of September, however, the German army was running out of steam. "The men stagger forward, their faces coated with dust, their uniforms in rags . . . like living scarecrows," wrote one German officer. When the Germans swung east to encircle the French and British armies, the Allies counterattacked.

The battle of the Marne raged along a front of 150 miles (240 kilometers) and lasted for five days (September 6 to 10). The Allied armies pushed north into gaps between the German units while fresh troops from Paris, brought to the front by a fleet of taxis, attacked from the south. The German army was forced to retreat to the River Aisne, where the troops dug defensive trenches. "Your Majesty, we have lost the war," Moltke told Kaiser Wilhelm.

Paintings such as this one of the last gun of the British Royal Horse Artillery's L Battery holding off the German advance at Néry (September 1, 1914) emphasize the courage and heroism of the soldiers while protecting those at home from the true brutality of war.
Far left: *This Belgian soldier wears a black shako (hat) and a heavy greatcoat. His uniform is one of the most old-fashioned in western Europe.*

The Eastern Front

Schlieffen had expected Russia to take ten weeks to get ready to fight. The Russians mobilized within ten days. In response to an urgent request from France, the Russian First Army, under General Paul Rennenkampf, invaded eastern Germany, defeating the Germans at the battle of Gumbinnen on August 20, 1914, and sending them into retreat. Maintaining radio contact, a second Russian army, under General Alexander Samsonov, attacked from the south. The danger to the German Eastern Front was so great that Moltke had to detach three corps from his army in the west and send them east. This move created the gaps in the German western line that allowed the Allies to defeat them at the battle of the Marne; according to the German general Erich von Falkenhayn, the Russians had saved France from total defeat.

Then came disaster for the Russians. Rennenkampf sent a radio message to Samsonov with details of his movements. The Germans intercepted the message, which was not in code. Knowing the exact positions of the Russian armies, the Germans transported their men by rail and defeated Samsonov at Tannenberg (August 23 to 31). Samsonov's army was driven back into a swamp and completely destroyed. One German eyewitness described the scene: "So fearful was the sight [of the drowning army] that, to shorten their agony, the Germans turned the machine guns on them. . . . And the mowing down of the cavalry brigade, 500 men on white horses, all killed and packed so closely that they remained standing." The Russians lost 125,000 men, the Germans only 13,000. Samsonov committed suicide. A fortnight later, again using the railways to transport their troops, the Germans surrounded and destroyed Rennenkampf's army; 100,000 Russians died.

At this point, the Russian chief of staff complained that he had been defeated because Russia was inadequately prepared for war: "At least one-third of the men had no rifle. These poor devils had to wait patiently . . . until their comrades fell be-fore their eyes and they could pick up their arms." Modern historians believe that although there may have been some shortages of weaponry and supplies, the Russian chief of staff was primarily attempting to blame someone else for Russia's defeats.

Despite these two bitter losses, Russians elsewhere were fighting well. In East Prussia in September, they overran a part of the Austrian army, which lost more than 300,000 men. The Germans had to create a new army (the IXth) to meet the threat. In October, again at the request of the French, the Russians attacked the German army in Poland. This time the battle was more evenly balanced and for a while the Germans were forced to retreat.

Cossack cavalry, frontiersmen from the south of Russia, assemble in 1914.
Left: *Few Russian soldiers are as well equipped as this young infantryman in winter uniform.*

Trench Warfare

The German VII Reserve Corps, pursued by the British Expeditionary Force during the battle of the Marne, dug the first trenches of the war. From the trenches, the Germans were able to halt the Allied advance. There followed what historians call the race to the sea; both armies marched north, trying to outflank (get around behind) each other, digging more trenches as they went. By the winter of 1914, the Western Front had become a narrow "ribbon of death," 475 miles (765 kilometers) long, stretching from the Belgian coast to Switzerland. The land between the two lines of trenches was called No Man's Land.

A typical trench was about ten feet (three meters) deep. The French used wattle revetments (reinforcements) to stop the walls from caving in; the British and Germans used sandbags, corrugated iron, and wood.

Trenches were built in a zigzag, forming a series of separate bays to limit the effect of shells bursting in the trenches and to stop the enemy from firing all the way along a trench if they captured part of it. Communication trenches stretched back to headquarters. Saps (short cul-de-sacs) poked out into No Man's Land to establish listening posts.

During 1915 and 1916, the generals on both sides tried to find a way to break through the lines of enemy trenches. But whereas each army had telephones, observation planes, machine guns, and railways to help them in their defense, their men still had to attack on foot, with rifles and bayonets. As the historian A. J. P. Taylor pointed out, the armies had a 20th-century method of defense but a 19th-century method of attack. The result was that every advance against the heavily defended enemy trenches involved slaughter on a scale never before known.

In early 1915, the French lost 240,000 men while recapturing a handful of villages in Champagne. A British initiative at Neuve-Chapelle that spring was stopped by two German units with a dozen machine guns; the British troops, ordered to attack "regardless of loss," suffered 13,000 casualties.

CHANGING ATTITUDES

Each soldier reacted in his own way to the pressures of trench warfare. Some found and enjoyed the excitement and comradeship they had anticipated: "I adore war. . . . It's all the best fun one ever dreamed of," wrote Julien Grenfell.

But for others, the apparent futility of trench warfare began to change their image of war. Victors no longer seemed like heroes; victims — the men who went "over the top" to their deaths — earned admiration and sympathy. Many soldiers were bitter, angry, and depressed. "Heavy artillery fire continued through the night and the list of wounded grows ever bigger. Bad drinking water . . . I have got stomach pains and diarrhea. It is torture. . . . Everybody is asking when we are going to be relieved," complained a German soldier. When the last member of British rifleman E. Chapman's platoon was killed (by a piece of shell that sliced off his head), Chapman found himself alone: "Giving up all hope of survival and feeling hopping mad, I waited with my Lewis gun for the enemy to come over the top." And it was always possible,

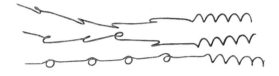

as the French novelist Henri Barbusse described in 1917, to come upon a wounded soldier standing upright, rooted to the spot, terrified, "a sort of screaming tree."

Many soldiers found that "it is worse than useless to think about things" and simply tried, as one French soldier wrote, "to carry oneself correctly." Others "switched off" from the horror around them and wrote home using the cheerful platitudes they might have read in the newspapers.

The two main killers on the Western Front are artillery, such as the British 13-pounder gun (below), and machine guns, like the German Maxim, which can fire 500 rounds a minute (far left). To hamper infantry movement, soldiers have hung barbed wire on iron screw pickets everywhere (above).

Life in the Trenches

The slaughter on the battlefields of the Western Front was so great that it comes as a surprise to discover that some soldiers on the quieter sections never saw the enemy at all. The diary of Charles Carrington of the British Royal Warwickshire Regiment shows that in 1916 he spent only 65 days in the front line and 36 in the support trenches — as compared with 120 days in reserve, 73 at rest, 10 in the hospital, and 17 on leave. He saw action only five times — one attack, two bombardments, one unsuccessful raid, and once when his unit held the line while other troops advanced.

A soldier's life in the trenches was spent not so much in fighting but in an endless, exhausting round of physical labor. The day began and ended with a "stand to" in case the enemy chose to make a dawn or dusk attack. The rest of the day was divided into "watches." Time was spent doing sentry duty or fatigues — digging and repairing trenches, fetching rations and stores — and trying to get some sleep. The busiest time was at night, when the men repaired the

barbed wire and patrolled No Man's Land to observe the enemy and rescue the wounded under the cover of darkness.

French officers relax in their living quarters, which have been dug out of the side of a trench. Here they receive an endless stream of orders, some of them as trivial as reminding them to sew on their buttons with their insignia the correct way up. Allied dugouts are temporary shelters with bunks, a table, and perhaps a few home comforts that the men have brought with them. The roof is made of corrugated iron but does not keep out the rain. In contrast, the Germans regard the front line as the new border of the German state, and their soldiers build concrete-lined bunkers up to 30 feet (9 meters) below ground level; some even have electric lighting, wallpaper, and carpets.

Below: *German soldiers use an adapted bicycle to generate electricity for radio signaling.*

"A Little Wet Home"

I've a little wet home in a trench,
Where the rainstorms continually drench;
There's the sky overhead,
Clay or mud for a bed,
And a stone that we use for a bench.
— Private Michael Riley

For the ordinary soldier, trench life was anything but comfortable. Rain and mud were frequent problems, especially in Flanders. Between October 25, 1914, and March 10, 1915, there were only 18 days there without rain. The trenches filled up with water: "It'll be all right as long as the U-boats [submarines] don't torpedo us," one German soldier joked. Soldiers were transformed into "statues of clay." Sometimes sleeping men sank into the mud and were never seen again; 15 men from one British Guards battalion drowned in the mud during the winter of 1914 to 1915.

The winter of 1916 to 1917 was one of the harshest in European history. British troops were issued leather jerkins and waterproof capes; the French stuffed newspapers and rags down their uniforms. Constantly wet and cold, the men's feet became diseased. There were 75,000 cases of trench foot, a painful condition resembling frostbite, in the British army during the war.

Sanitary arrangements were particularly unhealthy. Under fire, men simply relieved themselves in the nearest crater. In the British army, "Dan the sanitary man" (they were all called Dan, no matter what their real names were) came down the trenches each day, spraying creosote as a disinfectant. The hundreds of human corpses, however, made disease inevitable. In one part of the line "the stench was horrible, for . . . with all the shellfire . . . the whole place was a mess of filth and slime and bones and decomposing bits of flesh." In another, a human arm stuck out of the side of the trench; everybody who passed it solemnly shook it by the hand. The trenches were infested with flies, fleas, mosquitoes, and lice hopping from one body to another. Huge "corpse rats" thrived on the human flesh; the men used to tempt them out with hunks of stale bread, then kill them with their spades.

In fact, the conditions in which the men lived in the trenches were so terrible, they caused as many casualties as did the battles the men fought.

Ordinary French and British soldiers do not have dugouts; they curl up in "funk holes" scooped out of the sides of the trenches. "Duckboards" have been laid on the floor of this British trench to make a walkway over the mud. One soldier (second from right) cleans his Lewis gun. Above: A note on the back of this photograph, which shows German soldiers in a trench in 1914, suggests that it ought not to be published in the newspapers, as "our soldiers do not appear to have suitable shelter from the winter weather."

Casualties

No one knows for certain how many men were killed or injured during the First World War. Historians estimate that 1.3 million French soldiers died and 4.3 million were wounded — nearly 75 percent of France's mobilized forces. They believe 2 million German soldiers were killed and more than 4 million wounded (54 percent); the figures for the combined forces of the British Empire were probably 1 million killed and 2 million wounded (33 percent). As the war dragged on, governments gradually stopped publishing casualty figures.

If they were able to move, those who were wounded during a battle took refuge in shell craters. Every soldier carried a "field dressing" — a large gauze pad attached to a bandage that he would use to stanch the blood while he waited to be rescued or tried to get to the regimental aid post by "crater hopping" from one shell hole to the next. In these terrifying circumstances, some men showed great heroism. The English writer Robert Graves told of a friend who had been shot and lay groaning a short distance from the front line. Three men were killed and four men wounded trying to get to him. When a rescue party eventually reached him, they found he had "forced his knuckles into his mouth to stop himself crying out and attracting any more men to their death." Men who were not rescued often bled to death or were captured or killed by enemy soldiers.

When a battle quieted, stretcher parties went out. They carried bandages, scissors, plasters, iodine (an antiseptic), and morphine (a painkiller). Sometimes they were under orders, however, to bring back only those who had a chance of recovering.

Not all casualties occurred in battle. On the front line during November and December 1916, Charles Carrington's battalion never saw a German soldier — but during that time, snipers killed or wounded 50 men. Continual artillery fire, also a constant danger, caused psychological symptoms such as panic attacks and shaking in many soldiers; for a long time, though, the British army refused to accept that shell shock, as this condition came to be known, existed.

The Allied troops give the casualty clearing stations affectionate names such as Bandagehem and Mendinghem. Many of the nurses, known to Britons as VADs (from Voluntary Aid Detachments) or FANYs (First Aid Nursing Yeomanry), are young women volunteers eager to help with the war effort or alleviate the soldiers' suffering. Some of the orderlies are conscientious objectors.

In the filthy wartime conditions, blood poisoning and gangrene set in quickly; one-third of all battle casualties die. "When I undressed, my clothes reeked of pus," writes one nurse.

Nevertheless, medical knowledge advances during the war, especially in the development of artificial limbs (right), which are fitted when disabled men return home. Doctors also discover how to give a blood transfusion without causing the blood to clot.

A Time to Rest

Troops in reserve a few miles behind the lines theoretically had time to rest. British soldiers, however, were required to continue training, and they spent a great deal of time marching around the square, or "square bashing," to keep fit (to the jeers of the Australians and Canadians, who had much more freedom). Officers of all armies kept the troops busy with tasks such as mending roads, polishing their boots and buttons, and looking after the horses' harnesses. Whenever possible, the men spent time "chatting" — running a candle along the seams of their clothing to kill the lice.

Even the most enthusiastic officers realized, however, that the men could not train all day, so they arranged interunit soccer games and sports competitions. A soldier who showed any athletic ability whatsoever was liable to be told to represent his division, so a small, wiry sprinter might find himself fighting a great bear of a man in a boxing match. Other entertainments included reviews and pantomimes. One Brit-

ish review written in 1917 was set 50 years later, in 1967; it showed the war still being fought — by the soldiers' grandchildren. Sometimes the regimental band would play or a professional entertainer would come to put on a show for the troops.

Church was not very popular. One chaplain who asked the men, "So are you going to fight God's war?" received the weary reply, "Don't you think you ought to keep your poor Friend out of this bloody mess?"

Soldiers who had been able to obtain a pass would visit the local village. There they could buy souvenirs to send home to their families or sing and play cards all night in a café.

The soldiers longed for leave; yet when they were allowed to return home for a visit, many felt curiously estranged from their families, who had no real understanding of the horrors they had experienced. People seemed to want to hear about the gruesomeness of battle:

> But it ain't worthwhile to tell 'em:
> You might talk till all was blue.
> But you'll never make them compris
> What a bloke out there goes through.

Nevertheless, when it was time to return to the front, many men wept.

British soldiers play cards on a pile of "toffee apples"
(trench mortar bombs) in 1916.
Left: *British West Indian troops clean their rifles.*
Above: *A German soldier has made this musical instrument out of a bit of wood and an old tin can.*

The Widening War

During the early months of battle, what had started out as a conflict between the major European powers became a world war.

In the Pacific, Japan entered the war almost immediately, on August 23, 1914, capturing German colonies in the Caroline and Marshall islands. In September, with the help of British and Indian troops, the Japanese captured Qingdao, a German-controlled port city in China. British Empire troops from New Zealand took the island of Samoa from Germany on August 30, and within a month, Australian troops had occupied German New Guinea.

Most German colonies in Africa fared no better. On August 26, a Franco-British army conquered Togoland, and in September, South African forces invaded German Southwest Africa. In November, however, a force of Indian and British troops were unsuccessful when they attacked German East Africa. Paul von Lettos-Vorbeck, a German general there, would continue fighting on, undefeated, a month after the war ended two years later!

Some historians suggest that the Allies attacked German colonies "to eliminate a trading rival," but it was also important to capture German ports to ensure Allied control of the sea.

OPENING UP NEW FRONTS

Control of the sea was also an issue when Turkey entered the war on the German side in November 1914. The German government gave two cruisers — the *Goeben* and the *Breslau* — to the Turks, whereupon the crews put on red fezes and attacked Russian ports in the Black Sea.

The Turks closed the Dardanelles, the straits between the Black Sea and the Mediterranean, which gave access to Russia's only warm-water port. They also sent their Third Army to invade Russia, but many of the soldiers froze to death in the Caucasus Mountains. In February 1915, Turkish troops mounted an unsuccessful attack farther south, on the Suez Canal, threatening Britain's link with its colonies in India and the Far East.

In May 1915, the Allies persuaded Italy to enter the war on their side and to attack Austria. Between June 1915 and August 1917, 15 Italian divisions attacked the five defending Austrian divisions 11 times, gaining just 7 miles (11 kilometers) of ground.

Meanwhile, the British first lord of the admiralty, Winston Churchill, believed that a better plan would be to attack the Dardanelles and then strike north through the Balkans. After a failed attempt to force a passage through the straits in March 1915, an Allied force of British, Australian, New Zealand, and French troops landed on the Gallipoli peninsula on April 25, 1915.

The attack was a shambles from the start. The Turkish troops, strongly dug in on the cliffs and ridges above the beaches, immediately pinned the Allied troops down. When on August 6 a second assault of 20,000 Allied troops landed at Suvla Bay with not a Turkish soldier in sight, the British commander decided he could have a bath and an afternoon nap. By the time he was ready to proceed, his men faced vast Turkish reinforcements. Gallipoli turned into a trench war similar to that on the Western Front, with the added miseries of oppressive heat, cholera, and malaria, followed by a bitterly cold winter. In October 1915, Sir Charles Monro took over command of the Allied troops and recommended withdrawal.

The successful Turkish defense of Gallipoli meant that the British would have to fight the Turks on three other fronts — diverting troops and resources from the Western Front at enormous cost. One force started to fight its way up through Palestine from Egypt, and a second force began to work its way up from the Persian Gulf through Mesopotamia. Also, a number of military advisers were sent to help the Arabs who were rebelling against the Turks; one of these advisers was the famous Captain T. E. Lawrence (Lawrence of Arabia).

Elsewhere the war was also going badly for the Allies. In September 1915, German and Bulgarian troops attacked Serbia; on the Eastern Front, the Germans pushed the Russians out of Poland and the Baltic states of Estonia, Latvia, and Lithuania. In Berlin, German politicians planned a huge German empire in eastern Europe.

Allied troops land at Anzac Cove, Gallipoli.
Left: *A Turkish soldier prepares to face them.*

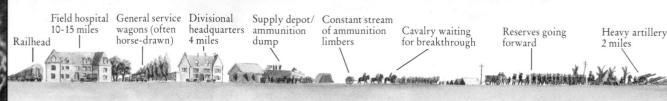

A TYPICAL TRENCH SYSTEM, 1917 (showing approximate distances from the front line)

Railhead | Field hospital 10-15 miles | General service wagons (often horse-drawn) | Divisional headquarters 4 miles | Supply depot/ ammunition dump | Constant stream of ammunition limbers | Cavalry waiting for breakthrough | Reserves going forward | Heavy artillery 2 miles

Position Warfare

On the Western Front, meanwhile, the trench system was growing more extensive; historians estimate that by 1918 there were 15,000 miles (24,000 kilometers) of trenches. The British army, which had some 2,500 shovels in 1914, had 10,638,000 by the end of the war. Every army found that as fast as it could dig trenches, canals, and field drains, shelling would destroy the work; whole areas turned back into marshland. Shelling also created craters that both sides fought to take. British army orders stated that every crater within 60 yards (55 meters) of a trench had to be captured — and new trenches had to be dug to it.

By 1915, people had realized that the war on the Western Front was not going to be won in one moment of military breakthrough. Both sides developed a military strategy that the German general Falkenhayn called position warfare: Armies refused to give up ground, whatever the cost. The war became one of attrition (wearing down). Attacks continued, but the objectives were less ambitious than they had once been. The French general Joseph Joffre described his tactics: "I nibble away at them." The battle of the Somme cost the lives of 420,000 British soldiers and 200,000 Frenchmen; but by the end of the battle, 450,000 Germans had died and

the German general Erich Ludendorff admitted, "The army had been fought to a standstill and was utterly worn out."

In 1916, General Falkenhayn launched an assault on the French fortress of Verdun. He calculated that for every two lives his army lost, the French should lose five. The fighting lasted ten months. In all, 282,323 Germans and 315,000 French soldiers died; the French called the road to Verdun the Voie Sacrée ("Holy Way") because so many men went down it to their deaths.

At the time of the war and for many years afterward, it was popularly believed that the generals of the First World War were men of limited intelligence who — living in luxury 20 miles (30 kilometers) from the front — were isolated from reality and needlessly caused the deaths of millions of men. Recently, however, historian John Terraine has argued that the generals were not the

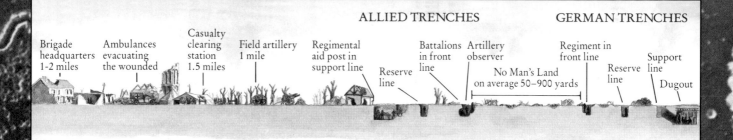

fools they are claimed to have been. They worked hard, often from 8:30 A.M. until 10:30 P.M., and they traveled constantly. They were quick to introduce new technology and try new strategies.

Terraine argues that, given the technology of the time, there was no strategic alternative to position warfare. The French general Robert Nivelle's failed attempt to break through the German lines in April 1917 proves that position warfare could work. The Germans had pulled back to new, stronger defenses (the Hindenburg line), where their position was so secure that the French lost 187,000 men advancing less than 3 miles (5 kilometers). French morale collapsed. The French army suffered

151 incidents of mutiny in 54 different divisions; at one point only two reliable units stood between the Germans and Paris.

Whether or not there was an alternative to a war of attrition, however, on many parts of the Western Front the war became just an endless string of murderous attacks.

Background: *In 1917, a network of trenches (seen here from the air) scar the earth near Loos. By now, the system (diagramed above) has become a vast muddle of multiple lines of trenches to which soldiers fall back if the enemy has captured the front line. In some places, No Man's Land might be as little as seven feet (two meters) wide, and sometimes German and Allied soldiers share the same trench, separated only by a wall of sandbags and barbed wire. On one occasion, British forces capture a German soldier who walks into their trench carrying his officer's breakfast on a tray.*
Far left: *German soldiers unload shells from a train.*
Left, above: *Wounded German and British soldiers wait to be evacuated, March 1918.*
Below: *German artillery crosses a trench bridge in June 1918. Brushwood hides the gun from aerial reconnaissance.*

Attack!

The assault that the British launched on the first day of the battle of the Somme (July 1, 1916) was typical of the First World War's frontal attacks. It was preceded by an artillery bombardment; in eight days 1,537 British guns fired 1,723,873 rounds. The bombardment was meant to reduce the enemy trenches to chaos and kill enemy soldiers. In fact, the Germans were relatively safe in their bunkers deep in the chalk of the Somme.

The British had dug mines (tunnels) under the German trenches and packed them with explosives; these were detonated just before the attack. The shock waves traveling through the ground broke the leg of a waiting British soldier. Then, at 7:30 A.M., with a blast on a whistle, the officers sent their men "over the top."

Along a front of 12 miles (20 kilometers), the men of 14 divisions leapt up and started to cross No Man's Land. Thinking that the bombardment would have completely destroyed the Germans, and hoping to prevent chaos among their little-trained volunteer recruits, the British commanders ordered their men to walk across No Man's Land in straight lines. The result was slaughter. "They went down in their hundreds. You didn't have to aim, we just fired into them," wrote one German machine-gunner.

At this point a British commander decided to explode a mine that had failed to detonate; this ended up burying the advancing British attackers under rock and soil. "Men were falling right and left of me, screaming above the noise of the shellfire and machine guns. . . . No man in his right mind would have done what we were doing," commented one British soldier.

Men battled through the bodies of their comrades, many of which were hanging, riddled with bullets, on the German barbed wire. One battalion was unable to advance because the soldiers could not climb over the heaped bodies of the dead and wounded blocking their way.

Some troops reached the German line and advanced down the trenches, throwing hand grenades into each bay as they came to it. But No Man's Land was so dangerous that it was impossible for their army to give them any support, and by nightfall most of the early gains had been lost. British casualties on the first day of the Somme were 20,000 dead and more than 35,000 wounded.

British soldiers go "over the top." The Germans immediately recognize the officer (top, center), as only he carries a pistol. Each private carries an anti-gas helmet, a groundsheet, a field dressing, an entrenching tool, 150 rounds of ammunition, and such extras as empty sandbags or a roll of barbed wire. Triangles of reflective tin attached to the men's knapsacks show the commanders how far the attack has advanced.

Russia: Victory and Defeat

The year 1916 was disastrous for the Allies. On the Western Front they suffered the losses of the battles of Verdun and the Somme. On April 24, in Dublin, a rebellion of Irish nationalists (supplied with German weapons) distracted the British from the war. Five days later, in Mesopotamia, an entire British division of 9,000 men surrendered to the Turks.

As in 1914, the Russians intervened to help their allies. Where the British had failed, Russian troops successfully invaded Turkey. Then, in June 1916, the Russian general Alexei Brusilov attacked Austrian troops in eastern Europe at 20 different points. The Austrian lines collapsed. Brusilov advanced 100 miles (160 kilometers) in a month, and he took 250,000 prisoners. Soon after, the Russian army inflicted a number of defeats on the Germans in the Balkans. More than 100 trains carried German troops from the Western Front to face the Russian threat before Brusilov was driven back.

Despite the military victories the army achieved, the strain of losses and fighting proved too great for the Russian government. The number of casualties on the Eastern Front was even greater than on the Western Front. One estimate suggests that 6.7 million Russian soldiers were killed or wounded. In September 1915, Czar Nicholas had gone to the front to take personal command of the armies, leaving his wife and the "mad monk" Rasputin in charge of the government. Strikes and demonstrations took place all over Russia, but the army refused to put them down. Russian soldiers began to desert in large numbers. On March 15, 1917, the czar abdicated. The provisional government that took over tried to continue the war but faced the same problem of domestic unrest, particularly after the Germans smuggled the Bolshevik (Communist) revolutionary Vladimir Lenin into Russia in April.

While the Russian government focuses on the war, problems in Russia itself increase. In July 1917, Cossack troops loyal to the provisional government fire machine guns on rioting workers.

Below: *Russian soldiers of 1917 shelter in the German trench they have just captured.*

Gas!

The First World War saw rapid advances in the military technology used by both sides, although generally the Germans were more innovative than the Allies. In 1914, they were the first to use machine guns and flamethrowers and to equip snipers with rifles that had telescopic sights.

In early 1915, the Germans set up a special scientific unit, Pioneer Regiment 36. Its commander, Fritz Haber, believed that "the Western Fronts, which were all bogged down, could only be got moving again by means of new weapons." He was eager to try one particular weapon scientists had just developed: At Ypres on April 22, 1915, a division of French colonial troops noticed a greenish yellow cloud drifting toward them. Throwing down their weapons, they ran for their lives. The cloud was chlorine gas, a lung irritant. The symptoms of gas poisoning were bright red lips and a blue face. Many of those affected died a slow death by suffocation. British and Canadian troops who replaced the French soldiers spent the night with towels over their mouths, listening to the gasping of soldiers dying in No Man's Land. "I'll tell you this much," one of them wrote later, "I might not have been wounded in body but I was wounded in my mind."

Many believed chlorine gas broke the 1907 Hague Convention restriction against weapons that caused unnecessary suffering,

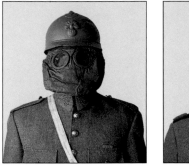

skin, and ripped out the lining of their lungs. The effects were so painful that mustard-gas patients often had to be strapped to their hospital beds, "screaming to die, the entire layer of the skin burned from face and body."

Although the Allies initially denounced the use of gas, by September 1915, they too were using it. After the development of the gas mask, gas killed few men (93 percent of those stricken were eventually able to return to duty), but both sides used gas to unsettle defenders during an attack.

and there was an outcry. A medical officer who arrived to treat the wounded wanted "to go straight away at the Germans and to throttle them." To the French, it was an example of German "scientific barbarism"; and even though the United States remained neutral at this point, many Americans were shocked and angry. The historian Basil Liddell Hart has argued that gas was a humane form of warfare, as it did not cause many deaths, but the general feeling among the troops was that it would be better to die suddenly than to endure the "awful agony" that chlorine gas produced.

Despite the outcry, the Germans continued to develop their new weapon. In December 1915, they added to the chlorine a more powerful suffocating gas, phosgene. After July 1917, the Germans also used mustard gas; it had no smell, and its effects went undetected for 9 to 12 hours. It temporarily blinded its victims, burned their

In 1918, the American artist John Singer Sargent paints Gassed, *a picture of soldiers temporarily blinded by gas making their way to a field hospital.*
Opposite page, left to right: *The first British pad respirators (May 1915) are made of cotton waste soaked in a soda solution. In July 1915, they are replaced by the "P" helmet, soaked in sodium phenate (and later hexamine) to make it gas-proof. In August 1916, the British introduce the box respirator, with a breathing tube attached to a canister filled with charcoal and absorbent chemicals. This design includes a nose clip, which means that the rubberized face piece does not need a "gas-tight" fit.*
Above left: *The French M2 mask (left), introduced in 1916, has a cotton gauze lining soaked in chemicals. The German* Leder- *mask of 1917 (right) has an oiled leather face piece and a filter, but it still relies on a "gas-tight" fit.*
Right: *Masks are also made for dogs that work as sentries, carry messages, and search for the wounded.*

Tanks

The British also designed a new weapon to break the stalemate of trench warfare. The idea for the weapon grew out of a plan to put machine guns on motorcycles; it was developed by the navy and designed by the Royal Naval Air Service. Shipped to France secretly as "water tanks," the new invention acquired the name it has had ever since. Because they had to be able to drive, the members of the first tank crews were mostly wealthy young men who had had cars in civilian life. They gave their machines names such as *Autogophaster*.

The British Mark I tank first entered the war on September 15, 1916, at the battle of the Somme. The Germans fled in terror when they saw the tanks approaching. Rumors spread that each one carried a crew of 400 men, had a speed of 30 miles (50 kilometers) per hour, and was made in Japan by Swedes. In fact, tanks proved to be good at running over machine guns, flattening barbed wire, and providing cover for advancing infantry, but they had a maximum speed of 4 miles (7 kilometers) per hour. They carried bundles of logs that they dropped into trenches to form bridges, yet the tanks frequently stuck in the mud or toppled over into craters. Inside, the tank crew of seven was cramped, hot, and suffocating in engine fumes. Working a tank was such a strain that during that first battle two tank commanders had nervous breakdowns, another shot himself because he felt he had failed, and a fourth went mad and shot his engine because it would not go fast enough.

At Cambrai on November 20, 1917, tanks fought for the first time in a massed

tactical formation: groups of three advanced with aircraft support. They broke through German lines and captured 5 miles (8 kilometers) of territory. But the big machines were still mechanically unreliable. Enemy fire destroyed 65 of the 378 tanks — but 114 were lost through breakdowns or accidents. In the battle of Amiens (August 8 to 12, 1918), Allied commanders had 342 tanks available on the first day, 145 on the second, 85 on the third, 38 on the fourth, and 6 on the last. Tanks were not yet the "war-winning weapon" the Allied generals had hoped they would be.

Other armies soon began to use tanks as well. The Germans used captured British vehicles and built 20 of their own A7V tanks, although these were slow and clumsy, requiring a crew of 18 men. By the end of the war, the French had 4,800 Schneider and Renault tanks. Further tech-

nological advances were still needed to make tanks really effective, but a new way of warfare was beginning to develop.

Inside this tank, the officer (far left) gives orders to the gunners (left and right) and the driver (top right). They share the cramped space with a carrier pigeon, who will bear any messages they need to send.
Below: *A British Mark IV tank in France in 1918.*

The War in the Air

In 1914, only 11 years after the first air flight, all the major powers had small military air forces. The Germans had 246 airplanes and the French had 156. The British had just 70 planes fit for service.

Initially, airplanes were used only for reconnaissance (observation). Then German and Allied airmen started to try to kill each other—at first simply with shotguns. A technological war developed. In May 1915, Antony Fokker, a Dutch aircraft designer who had a factory in Germany, invented an interrupt mechanism that allowed German pilots to fire machine guns between the blades of their propellers. Also, the Germans developed tactics for dogfights; these included the Immelmann turn, named after a German pilot, which involved looping the loop and coming up behind a pursuing airplane. These advances, along with the German Albatross and the Fokker Triplane, gave the Germans almost unbroken control of the air.

During "bloody April" in 1917, the British Royal Flying Corps (RFC) had three times as many airplanes as the Germans, yet 316 RFC crewmen were killed; the average flying life of a new recruit was just 17 hours. Later the same year, however, German air dominance was finally broken when the Allies began to fly Sopwith Camels (so named because they carried their guns in a hump behind the engine) and Nieuport and Spad fighter planes.

German pilots fought in groups, called circuses. The most famous was that of Baron Manfred von Richthofen (whose red-painted plane earned him the nickname Red Baron). They patrolled the skies over the Western Front twice a day. The RFC made continuous flights from dawn to dusk. Many of their pilots went out alone on "hunting patrol," recklessly attacking the enemy whenever they met, whatever the odds.

The young pilots on both sides developed a special bravado. When one German pilot lost an expensive fur glove over a French air base, he returned the next day to drop the other one; the pilot who found the gloves flew over the German base and dropped a thank-you note. On Christmas Day 1914, the English pilot L. A. Strange bombed a German base with soccer balls for a joke. Another thrill was to go "sausage shooting"—attacking enemy observation balloons. Filled with hydrogen, the balloons exploded spectacularly, but it took a skilled pilot to avoid being struck by the blast.

Even the bravest pilots suffered from the constant psychological strain of combat. British pilots were not allowed to carry parachutes (they were thus forced to try to save their airplanes); the famous ace "Mick" Mannock carried a pistol so that he could kill himself if his plane caught fire. Mannock wept for his dead comrades and despised himself as a hired assassin. Even von Richthofen, who shot down 80 pilots and claimed "I am a hunter," admitted: "I am in wretched spirits after every battle." He was shot down and died behind Allied lines in 1918.

During a dogfight over France, a pilot glances anxiously back at his wounded rear gunner. In the distance, German Fokker Triplanes (identified by black crosses) battle with British Sopwith Camels (bearing red, white, and blue target markings). The German name for a pilot who has shot down ten enemy airplanes is Oberkanone ("top gun"). The French and British call a pilot an ace when he has shot down five airplanes.
Left: *Each airplane in von Richthofen's circus is brightly painted.*

43

Air Raids

In January 1915, the Germans mounted the first airship raid on England, bombing two towns in the southeast. Air raids soon became common up and down the battle lines.

At first, many people found the raids more fascinating than alarming; one British man declared the zeppelin (airship) to be "the biggest sausage I ever saw." Repeated raids, however, became frightening, especially as it was rumored that German spies were guiding the zeppelins with car headlights. In autumn 1915, a raid on a business district of London killed 38 people and caused extensive damage to property.

In the clouds, the zeppelins' crews stood (to save weight, no seats were allowed) and tried to locate their target: "It was rubbish to say this was the so-and-so building. . . . You were happy enough if you found London," remembered one crewman. Since the air raids began well before the British had developed effective fighter planes like the Sopwith Camel, zeppelin crewmen faced little danger. One Royal Naval Air Service pilot was sent up to stop an airship with a 12-bore shotgun; another was given fishhooks to drop on a zeppelin, in the hope that they would puncture its gasbag.

By the autumn of 1916, however, British airplanes were equipped with explosive

shells. On September 2, a British pilot shot down his first zeppelin, then immediately fired off his flare and looped the loop. After two more unsuccessful raids, the zeppelins stopped coming.

The air above Britain was not quiet, though. Since spring 1916, German Gotha planes had also been bombing Britain, and these raids continued.

Later, Britain retaliated with air raids against German industry, but the war ended before Britain could inflict heavy losses.

The German airship LZ 77 is 536 feet (163 meters) long. The hydrogen-filled gasbag gives it buoyancy, and the propellers on the back of the crews' gondolas give forward motion. This zeppelin will carry out raids over England

in September 1915, but it will be shot down over France in 1916.
Below: *The Germans mount air raids against the French throughout the war. Here civilians flee from bombed houses in Abbeville, France, in May 1918.*

The War at Sea

At the time of the First World War, Britain claimed its navy was the best in the world. It was the largest, but since the 1880s Germany had become a rival for control of the sea. In some ways German ships were superior; in particular they were better suited to the short-term voyages associated with battle than were English ships. In addition, the Germans had developed submarines known as U-boats (short for *Unterseeboot,* meaning "undersea boat").

As soon as war broke out, the British moved to blockade German ports; by pre-

venting any ships from entering its ports with supplies, they hoped to cripple Germany. The Germans, for their part, announced in early 1915 that they would use their U-boats to attack merchant ships trading with Britain.

In May 1915, a German U-boat sank the liner *Lusitania,* which, in addition to its passengers, was suspected of carrying munitions to Britain. In all, 1,198 people drowned; 128 were Americans. The United States exploded in anger, and President Wilson threatened Germany with war. In response, Germany promised that in the future its submarines would follow "cruiser rules" — that is, they would warn if they intended to attack a ship, to give the crew a chance to evacuate. But the advantage of U-boats lay in the element of surprise; when the U-boats did give a warning, some merchant ships tried to ram them. The British even disguised some heavily armed battleships to look like merchant ships in order to lure the U-boats into the open, where they were easily attacked. Angered by these attacks, the Germans returned to unrestricted submarine warfare in early 1916, but by April they had once again agreed to follow cruiser rules in response to American pressure.

THE BATTLE OF JUTLAND

At this point, Admiral Reinhard Scheer, the commander of the German High Seas Fleet, decided to engage the British navy. A fleet of battle cruisers went to Norway under Rear Admiral Franz von Hipper; its orders were to locate the British navy and lure it into a trap. However, the British had acquired a German radio codebook from a drowned sailor, and when they intercepted the message "Carry out secret instruction

2490," they realized that a major operation was about to begin. They, too, decided to trap the enemy, and they sent out battle cruisers under the command of Admiral Sir David Beatty to draw the German High Seas fleet toward the British navy. Hipper and Beatty sailed around in the North Sea looking for each other.

The two fleets met at 2:15 P.M. on May 31, 1916, and both fleets attacked, beginning the battle of Jutland — the only large-scale naval battle of the war. The British gunners were not as accurate as the Germans; two British battle cruisers exploded and sank, and another was put out of action. Admiral Beatty turned and fled, leading the main German fleet into the trap as planned. At 6:15 P.M., Admiral Scheer realized that the main British fleet was upon him. In a brilliant maneuver, the German fleet turned, laid down a smoke screen, and fired 28 torpedoes. A short, fierce battle followed. Night was falling, and Admiral Sir John Jellicoe, the commander of the main British fleet, knew that he was (as the future English prime minister Winston Churchill put it) "the only man who could lose the war in an afternoon." He disengaged from the battle, and the Germans returned safely to port.

No one has ever been able to decide who won the battle of Jutland. The British lost more ships and men, but the German fleet never left port again. Perhaps the best assessment of the battle came from an American reporter: "The German Fleet has assaulted its jailer but is still in jail."

THE U-BOAT PERIL

Bad harvests throughout Europe in 1916 had made food imports vital, and Russia's domestic political problems encouraged the German government to think that with a final push it could win the war. On February 1, 1917, the German government reintroduced unrestricted submarine warfare, sending out an order: "To all U-boats — sink on sight." In the period from February to December 1917, German submarines sank 2,966 Allied and neutral ships carrying food, munitions, or men to Allied countries. One in four ships leaving British ports was sunk. "Can the army win the war before the navy loses it?" wondered one British admiral.

In late summer 1917, British merchant ships began to sail in convoy, escorted by warships. Patrols of hunting vessels destroyed the U-boats with depth charges and the British developed an effective sea mine (by copying German mines). The U-boats had lost control of the sea.

An Allied navy ship, painted in an abstract pattern meant to serve as camouflage, lays a smoke screen to protect a convoy.
Left: *The torpedo room of a German U-boat, 1917.*
Above: *A model of the British warship HMS* Conqueror.

Enter America

The warring European powers all sought support from the United States — where money, supplies, and young men of fighting age were plentiful — but for a long time Americans did not want to go to war. The United States had traditionally kept out of international politics; when war broke out in Europe, President Wilson instructed his country to be "impartial in thought as well as in action." Many Americans saw the war as Britain's attempt to expand its colonial and trading empire at Germany's expense. And American feminists opposed the war because they believed that it would increase male domination of society. But perhaps because English was a common language, many Americans sympathized with Britain and, consequently, the Allies.

During the war years, American nationalism and the call for involvement grew. Progressive (reforming) politicians in America imagined a "world somehow made permanently different by our participation" in world affairs. American businessmen saw the war as a "supreme opportunity for American manufacturers to gain worldwide markets." They resented the German U-boat campaigns, although it was true that the American trade was supplying the Allies and their armies. Throughout 1916, President Wilson encouraged Americans to discuss these issues.

On January 16, 1917, British Intelligence intercepted a telegram from the German foreign secretary, Arthur Zimmermann, offering Mexico an alliance — if Mexico would attack the United States. It was the last straw. On April 2, President Wilson declared that America had a duty "to make the world safe for democracy," and on April 6, 1917, the United States formally entered the war.

Across America, there was a wave of anti-German feeling. Hamburgers (originally named after a German town) were

now called liberty sandwiches, and one writer claimed that "men and women who teach the German language are traitors." Other ethnic groups also suffered in the campaign for "100 percent Americanism."

The War Industries Board was set up; for the first time, the United States government took control of industry, agriculture, and transport. It introduced conscription in order to raise an American expeditionary force; on June 5, 1917, ten million men registered themselves as available for military service.

It took more than a year to draft and train a million doughboys (infantrymen), but America's involvement in the war improved the Allies' morale immediately. In January 1918, President Wilson made his famous Fourteen Points address. In it he listed the principles on which he wanted to build peace after the war — including freedom of the seas, arms reductions, the right of nations to govern themselves, and the establishment of the League of Nations (through which nations could resolve their differences without having to go to war). The Fourteen Points gave the Allies a morale boost; they were not just fighting *against* the enemy, they were fighting *for* a better world.

American doughboys wave farewell from the deck of a troopship. When they arrive in Europe, British VAD nurse Vera Britten is surprised at how big and healthy they look as compared to European soldiers; to Britten, they seem "so godlike, so magnificent, so splendid . . . compared with the tired, nerve-racked men of the British army."
Below: *American sailors on parade spell out a message: "Long live France."*

Total War

The First World War was a total war; the conflict was not just between the armies on the battlefields but between entire nations. Civilians as well as soldiers suffered wherever the battle lines were drawn. Both sides sought to cripple each other's economies through the war at sea. In response, each nation had to mobilize its economy, as well as its soldiers, to sustain the war effort.

In September 1914, Britain ordered 1,792 machine guns from the armaments firm of Vickers, even though at that time the firm could make only 12 guns a week. In the early months of the war, shortages of high explosives meant that British industry could produce only 250 shells a day — a situation dubbed the "scandal of the shells" — which led to the fall of the government in May 1915. French industry was in an even worse condition. More than half of France's coal, iron, and steel had been produced in the northeast of the country, which was now under German control. Not only materials but also workers were in short supply. By June 1915, out of an active male population of 12.6 million, France had sent 5.6 million to the front. Even while the United States remained neutral, the Allies had to depend on American supplies for survival.

It was clear that the Allied countries needed government intervention and centralized planning. In Britain, the Defence of the Realm Act (1914) gave the British government the power to seize factories and buy any goods it wanted; in 1916 all wool, hay, and leather were commandeered for the army. It became illegal to work at nonessential trades such as house painting. It was also made illegal to talk about military matters, trespass on railways, buy binoculars, or light bonfires.

France appointed a Socialist, Albert

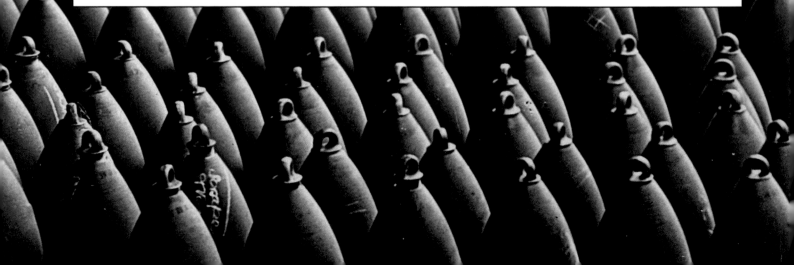

Thomas, as secretary of state for artillery and munitions. He organized French industry into groups of firms, with large companies such as Renault as group leaders. In this way, by discussion with a few leading industrialists, he could coordinate production. Firms employed women, children, disabled people, workers from French colonies, and prisoners of war to solve their employment problems. Thomas encouraged them to adopt more efficient "time and motion" principles of management, which increased production by 50 percent. By 1918, France was producing more armaments than any other country in Europe.

All the countries of Europe used private firms to supply their war needs. They also gave companies large sums of money to expand. These firms made huge profits; in France and Germany, this situation led to a number of serious political scandals. It became necessary to conduct investigations into some companies' accounts.

In all countries, after an initial burst of cooperation between the unions and the employers, the workers began to complain about poor wages and conditions. In 1917, inspired by the Russian Revolution, workers went on strike all over Europe; the countries that failed to deal with this situation would lose the war. France and Britain did best, setting up shop-steward systems in factories, which allowed the workers to have a say in how their factories were run. France also set a legal minimum wage and established an arbitration service to negotiate between employers and employees. In Britain, the government settled most wage demands simply by granting higher pay.

Shells are stacked ready for dispatch.
Above, left to right: *British munitions workers fill a shell (painted yellow to indicate high explosives), then add an adaptor ring to take the fuse. They paint a color-coded ring on the shell to indicate the type of explosive (in this case, green to indicate trotyl), then a red ring to show it has been filled. Finally, they screw a transit plug into the shell.*

Shortages

Eventually, the war brought shortages and suffering to all the belligerent countries; but it was not until 1917, after the bad harvest of 1916, that serious food shortages occurred and governments were forced to introduce rationing.

In Britain, wartime dislocation and U-boat attacks caused certain shortages right away. Meat, margarine, wheat, butter, and sugar (which had been made from German sugar beets) became scarce. "I am a slice of bread. . . . SAVE ME AND I WILL SAVE YOU!" government posters urged. In France, the main problem was a shortage of coal. Food production remained sufficient, although people were annoyed by rising prices and a government decision to fix the price of bread that pushed many bakers into bankruptcy. With the help of food supplies arriving from America, France and Britain kept their populations adequately fed throughout the war. Historians have discovered that the civilian death rate did not rise in France, and it actually fell in Britain (where rationing meant that food was more fairly distributed between rich and poor than ever before).

The Central Powers suffered worse problems. Lines were common; Anton Srmcka, who was a child in Austria-Hungary during the war, remembers standing in line to buy potatoes: "When the policeman came: finished! We'd stood there for half the night . . . and we hadn't got a thing." From 1916 until the end of the war, strikes in protest against high food prices were common.

The situation in Germany was even more serious; the ports were still blockaded, and little food could enter from other countries. The government nationalized wheat production, creating one office to buy grain and another to distribute it. The system failed completely. In October 1915, the Imperial Potato Office forbade farmers to use potatoes for fodder; as a result, farmers had to slaughter all their animals. By the winter of 1916 to 1917, not even potatoes were available—only fodder beets. During the following year, people lived on berries, nuts, nettles, and anything else they could find that was edible. The death rate rose steadily, especially among children. Workers, insufficiently fed, were too weak to work efficiently, and industrial production fell by 40 percent. The number of working days lost through strikes rose from 42,000 in 1915 to 2 million in 1917. By the end of 1917, Austria-Hungary and Germany were on the verge of collapse.

When the United States joined the war, Americans too were encouraged to save food. Children were excused from school in order to farm, and First Lady Edith Wilson planted a victory garden on the White House lawn.

The efforts of the 260,000 British young women who work on farms as laborers in the Women's Land Army keep production up in England.
Below: *In a typical week in 1917, rations for a British adult (right) and for a German adult (left) might seem unsatisfying.*

Women and the War

"Without women, victory will tarry," declared Britain's prime minister, Lloyd George. Women from all the belligerent countries went to the front as nurses; volunteers in the Women's Army Auxiliary Corps (WAAC) of the British Expeditionary Force worked as cooks, storekeepers, typists, carpenters, and drivers. A Signal Corps unit of 250 women fluent in French and English went to France as telephonists for the American Expeditionary Force. They complained that the newspaper and radio reports back home said "never a word about the . . . girls who plug from morning until night, who scream their lungs out over the lines."

On the home front, a good deal of the burden of war fell on women. Husbands went off to fight, leaving their wives to manage the family budgets, cope with ration books, raise the children, and deal with the authorities — in addition to carrying on their normal work.

The number of women working outside the home increased — in Britain, from just over three million to nearly five million. Working-class women delivered coal and worked as laborers. In both England and France, "munitionettes" made shells and weapons in factories. Middle-class women joined the Civil Service, worked as

conductors on trams, or became teachers. In Britain, a Women's Police Force formed; it proved especially good at preventing prostitution.

At the time, it was suggested that the war "revolutionized the industrial position of women" by giving them more freedom. Recently, however, historians have questioned this claim. Women worked because they needed the money. Most of the female war workers were working-class women who had always needed to work; they had lost their jobs as domestic servants, or in textile and clothing factories, because of wartime cutbacks by their employers. In France, women sought work because their husbands were away at the front and the family allowance (1.25 francs a day) was only half the usual wage paid to a woman. Only 3 out of 60 women interviewed by the British historian Deborah Thom said they wanted "to do their bit" for their country.

War propaganda glamorized women workers. In fact, the work was anything but glamorous. TNT dust poisoned the munitionettes and turned their skin yellow; they were known as canaries. The French writer Marcelle Capy described the "skinny, exhausted little girls [with] the ravaged faces of old women" who worked as laborers, moving up to 35 tons, 14 hours a day, 29 days a month. In Britain, one 16-year-old munitions worker was injured in the 26th hour of her shift; the judge dismissed the case brought against the firm on the grounds that "the most important thing in the world today is that ammunition shall be made." In the words of one French tradeunionist, women had simply been "delivered unto a holocaust."

One result of the terrible conditions was that, in Britain, the number of female tradeunion members increased 276 percent during the war. In France in 1917, there were a number of strikes by women workers — notably one that lasted 11 days at the de

Dion armaments factory near Paris.

After the war, most women workers were fired and told to serve their country by going home and having babies. In industries where women continued to be employed, they were confined to the less-skilled, lower-paid jobs. The war had failed to improve the employment situation for women. As one French woman complained in 1919: "My husband has been in the army for the last six years. I worked like a slave at Citroën during the war. I sweated blood there, losing my youth and my health. In January I was fired, and since then have been poverty stricken."

Women do dangerous, responsible, and physically demanding jobs on the home front, such as working in privately run factory fire services (left), but they are not paid as much as men, and men do not accept them as equals in the workplace.
Above: *Women work as radio and telephone operators for the British Royal Navy.*
Below: *A female soldier fights in the front line of the Russian army.*

Propaganda

All governments used propaganda to affect public opinion; the British government even created the secret War Propaganda Bureau. It had three sections: a political intelligence division (to find out the state of public opinion), a news division (to keep the public informed), and a cinema division. After 1917, the United States Committee on Public Information (CPI) ran a massive propaganda campaign; 75 million pamphlets were distributed and 75,000 speakers (the Four-minute Men) were sent to tour the country. The CPI made especially good use of films such as *The Kaiser: The Beast of Berlin*.

Governments monitored newspapers to ensure that they maintained morale. "My wound? It doesn't matter . . . but make sure you tell them that all Germans are cowards," the Catholic newspaper *Echo de Paris* reported a French soldier as saying. The Socialist newspaper *Le Midi* reported that "half the German shells are made of cardboard, and they don't even burst!" Also, a number of the postcards printed privately and for the government during the war were of the "patriotic fantasy" kind — for example, an idealized family pictured on a map of France, with the slogan "This is what you're fighting for." In France, priests, teachers, and local politicians urged all classes and parties to lay aside their differences. In Britain, posters reminded workers that strikes helped the kaiser.

Some propaganda was designed expressly to make people hate the enemy. German posters pictured Germany alone, surrounded by enemies. A full-page illustration in a French newspaper showed a German soldier giving his fiancée two rings — and they were still on the hand he had cut from a French woman. A notorious piece of British hate propaganda was the "corpse-conversion" story. It began in *The Times*, with an article based on a mistranslation of the German word *Kadaver*. The article falsely claimed that the Germans were boiling down the corpses of their dead soldiers, instead of animal carcasses, to obtain fats and oils.

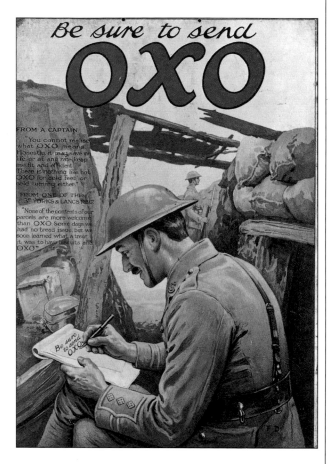

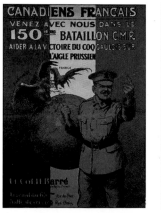

A great deal of pressure was put on those groups that might have undermined public support of the war. A poster campaign demanded that all Germans living in Britain should be arrested as potential spies. When in 1916 the British government introduced conscription, 16,000 conscientious objectors (who refused, on moral grounds, to fight) were treated harshly and imprisoned — although most "conshies" were eventually allowed to do other kinds of war work, such as driving ambulances. When the French writer Romain Rolland suggested that not all Germans were barbarians, he received a torrent of angry letters. Perhaps it is not surprising, then, that a strong peace movement never developed during the war.

By 1917, the success of government propaganda had begun to cause problems. The exaggerations of Allied military successes had led to the expectation of an early victory. As the war dragged on, there was a danger that disillusionment would set in. Governments realized that if people were to keep fighting, they needed to know what they were fighting for. Later propaganda, therefore, tended to stress that this was the "war to end all wars," and that after the war, the League of Nations and the new moral order in world politics that President Wilson of the United States proposed would ensure a lasting and just peace.

Some propaganda appeals to a sense of shame. The British poster being pasted up (right) asks, "Are YOU in this?" and juxtaposes soldiers, nurses, and workers with a shirker (hidden by the brush) who stands with his hands in his pockets.
Left, above: Not all propaganda is published by governments. This advertisement encouraging people to send soldiers Oxo beef stock cubes presents a romanticized view of trench life.
Left, below: This French Canadian poster (far left) appeals to nationalistic feelings, while an Italian cartoon (near left) shows the German kaiser trying to devour the world.

Last Days

In the winter of 1917, Austrian and German troops routed the Italians at the battle of Caporetto. Four hundred thousand Italian soldiers deserted and set off for home, looting as they went. In November, the British offensive at Passchendaele came to an end in a blizzard. Meanwhile, the provisional Russian government had collapsed. On December 15, 1917, the new Bolshevik government signed a truce with the Germans. After the Treaty of Brest-Litovsk (March 3, 1918), Russia withdrew from the war and gave up its claims to land in Poland, the Ukraine, and the Baltic states.

The Germans, free now to concentrate on the Western Front, were determined to win the war before the American troops arrived. They had the benefit of extra troops released from the Eastern Front. They also had new tactics; lightly equipped stormtroopers had been trained to make lightning attacks on weak points in the enemy line.

The offensives they launched were called by code names. Operation Michael began on March 21, 1918; under cover of fog, the Germans broke through the British line and advanced rapidly. The Germans followed this success up with Operation Georgette (April) and Operation Blücher (May), until they were only 55 miles (90 kilometers) from Paris.

By June, however, many German storm-troopers had been killed in the attacks, and their places were taken by boys and older men; Germany had run out of young men to send to war. Supplies failed to keep up with the troops, and German soldiers started looting.

At the same time, the American Expeditionary Force began to arrive in large numbers. Between April and July 1918, the Allied forces were joined by 950,000 American soldiers. On June 1, the Americans helped the French to stop a German advance at Château-Thierry.

On August 8, when the Allies launched their counterattack, many German soldiers surrendered; it was the German army's "black day." On September 12, British, Australian, and American forces broke through the German Hindenburg line. The German general Ludendorff had a nervous breakdown.

COLLAPSE

Everywhere, Allied forces were starting to defeat the enemy. In the Middle East, a British army under General Edmund Allenby fought its way up through Palestine. On October 1, 1918, an Arab force led by the Amir Feisal and T. E. Lawrence captured Damascus, and on October 30, Turkey signed an armistice with the Allies.

In the Balkans, Bulgaria surrendered in September, and on November 1, the Allies recaptured the Serbian capital, Belgrade. The Italians defeated the Austrian army at

the battle of Vittorio Veneto (October 24 to November 12).

The German and Austrian people had reached the end of their endurance. In Austria-Hungary, soldiers on leave began to refuse to return to the front, and they attacked army officers who challenged them. On November 3, 1918, Austria-Hungary surrendered, and nine days later the emperor abdicated. It was the end of the Austro-Hungarian Empire.

In Germany, striking workers demanded democracy and peace. The railway system collapsed; food-supply trains disappeared. On November 3, the German navy mutinied. On November 11, 1918, Germany signed an armistice that went into effect at 11 A.M. Except in East Africa, the First World War had come to an end.

German prisoners of war in Abbeville, France, 1918.
Above: *American soldiers arriving in France, 1918.*

Versailles and After

In June 1919, the victorious powers met at Versailles in France to decide the terms of the peace treaty. They decided to strip Germany of its colonies, air force, and navy, and to allow the humbled nation to keep only a tiny army of 100,000 men. The Germans were blamed for starting the war and were required to pay huge reparations — the exact amount, to be determined later, would include all costs the Allies had incurred in fighting.

In eastern Europe, the Austro-Hungarian Empire was broken up. Smaller states including Czechoslovakia and Yugoslavia (which included the former Austrian province Bosnia as well as what had been Serbia before the war) were established. In the Middle East, the Turkish Empire was replaced by smaller states, most under French and British administration. And in Africa and Asia, former German colonies came under the influence or rule of Britain or Japan.

The First World War was over, but its effects were to have long-reaching consequences. The weapons and tactics developed during the war — tanks, swift stormtrooper attacks with airplane support, aircraft carriers, and air raids — changed the nature of all future wars. The mobilization of the warring countries' economies stimulated economic growth in the armament, automobile, aircraft, and chemical industries and sparked industrialists to develop new management techniques. Women's contributions to the war effort raised new questions about their place in society. And in Britain, the idea of creating a "land fit for heroes" for soldiers to return to played an important part in the development of the welfare state.

As American industrialists and financiers had hoped in 1914, the United States emerged from the war as a leading economic power. During the war, American armament and engineering industries had quadrupled their output to supply the Allied armies, and after the war, American businesses continued to build on this foundation. Debate about America's role in foreign affairs continued after the war, but America's participation in the conflict and Woodrow Wilson's political vision began the process of creating a new role for the United States in international politics and diplomacy.

In Germany, the consequences of the war and the peace negotiated at Versailles were devastating. Many German soldiers failed to settle back into society, believing that they had been "stabbed in the back" by the civilian population. They formed a violent, drifting element of society on which Adolf

Hitler would draw when he recruited his Nazi stormtroopers in the 1930s. Broader German anger about the Treaty of Versailles, the blame laid on Germany, and the unreasonable reparations demanded by the Allies also contributed substantially to Hitler's rise and ultimately to the outbreak of the Second World War.

During the war, one British munitions worker had written, "The fact that I am using my life's energy to destroy human souls gets on my nerves. . . . But once the war is over, never in creation will I do the same thing again." But the peace negotiated at Versailles was fatally flawed, and twenty years after it was established it would collapse, forcing the world to face the suffering and devastation of war once again.

While the people of Paris celebrate the armistice on November 11, 1918 (above), impoverished Germans rely on soup kitchens (below), which become places of bitterness, argument, and political extremism.

How Do We Know?

A mass of material is available to the historian who wants to study the First World War. In particular, there are many primary sources (original documents dating from the time). After the German government published all its official papers from 1914, all the other countries of Europe except the new Soviet Union did the same. Historians can also consult wartime photographs, films, newspapers, posters, and advertisements, and the memoirs of such men

as the German general Erich von Falkenhayn and the Swedish writer Sven Hedin. To find out about the lives and opinions ordinary people had during the war, historians can read diaries (for instance, that of Charles Carrington) or letters home.

Historians must not, however, let themselves be misled by their sources. Memoirs sometimes fail to distinguish between what was true and what the writer wanted to be true. Many newspaper articles were simply pro-war propaganda, and official documents can sometimes give a very detached impression of events, an impression that does not reflect what actually happened to people.

Writers of the time were deeply affected by the war, and they produced some very moving work. The German-born American novelist Erich Maria Remarque, who wrote *All Quiet on the Western Front* in 1929, had been a soldier in the United States Army for a short while; his book is so realistic that a reader can easily forget it is fiction. The poems of Wilfred Owen and Siegfried Sassoon are so powerful that they in particular have affected the way we think about the First World War. They have produced a very dark image of the war. Many soldiers felt the need to put pen to paper, and though they often wrote about the distress war caused them, not all were as bitter as Sassoon and Owen. The poetry of some soldiers (such as Michael Riley) is just cheerful doggerel.

These written sources can be supplemented by the memories of people who were there — although these men and women are now very old and time may have changed their recollection of events. Their personal feelings may also have altered their memories. Historians have to remember, too, that an eyewitness sees only a tiny part of the whole story, and that his or her memories may not be typical. Nevertheless, British historians in particular have done a great deal of work in this area, and the descriptions in this book of conditions in the trenches, of the battle of the Somme, and of shortages in Austria all include the recorded memories of people present at the time. Since so much recorded oral (spoken) history is British, a historian studying these sources might easily get the impression that the British bore the brunt of the war. In fact, Britain did not do most of the fighting and did not suffer the greatest casualties, as anyone who visits the battlefields in France and looks at the names on the thousands of graves will see.

CAN THE CAMERA LIE?

Film is another important resource for historians; the warring governments commissioned photographers and filmmakers to document the war pictorially, and the commercial movie-making industry was quick to maximize the war's emotional and political interest. Some films, such as Charlie Chaplin's *Shoulder Arms*, were never meant to be taken seriously. Others, such as *Hearts of the World* (a film about the German invasion of Belgium), are clearly propaganda. However, it is disappointing to find out that much of the footage that seems to show actual battles was specially staged after the events.

Historians need to be careful how they use film. The British television series "The Great War" caused a furious debate when it was broadcast in the 1960s. Some scenes filmed on the battlefields during the war had been used in the wrong contexts to illustrate different events, and some footage had been shown back-to-front, so the British always came from the same side of the screen.

SECONDARY SOURCES

A mass of secondary material (written by historians after the events) is also available. Over 5,000 books have been written about the causes of the war — more than on any other topic in history. Some historians, such as A. J. P. Taylor and John Terraine, have contributed considerably to our understanding of the war. Others have not been so insightful and objective (fair).

The key problem is that it is virtually impossible to study the First World War objectively. It is hard to form an opinion of how good the generals were during the war after reading accounts of how the men suffered during an attack. And it is difficult to study the murder at Sarajevo without thinking of the recent troubles in Bosnia.

But then again, maybe it is not wrong to be affected by the story of the First World War. Many of the men who signed up and went to die did so because they genuinely wanted the First World War to be the "war to end all wars," to make the world a better place for future generations. They wanted to affect us.

Far left: *American and French war photographers.*
Near left: *Letters are sorted in a German field post office in 1918.*
Above: *Photographs such as this one of disabled German soldiers demonstrating in Berlin in 1918, and the many war cemeteries in France (below), remind us of the tremendous human cost of the war.*

Index

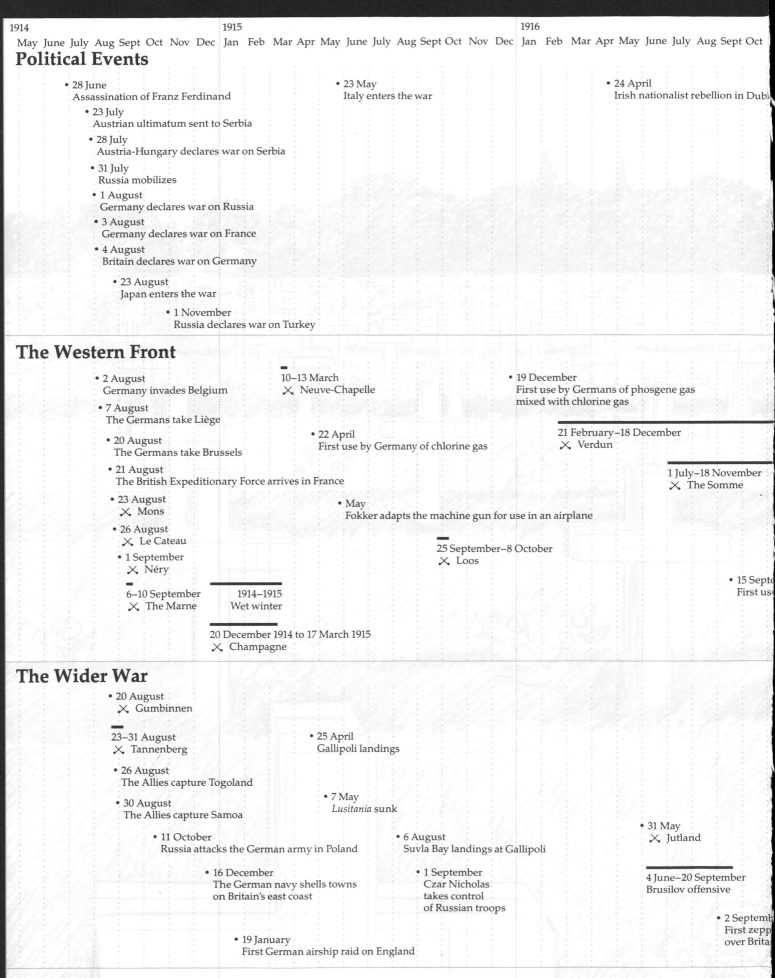

1914								1915												1916									
May	June	July	Aug	Sept	Oct	Nov	Dec	Jan	Feb	Mar	Apr	May	June	July	Aug	Sept	Oct	Nov	Dec	Jan	Feb	Mar	Apr	May	June	July	Aug	Sept	Oct

Political Events

- **28 June**
  Assassination of Franz Ferdinand

- **23 July**
  Austrian ultimatum sent to Serbia

- **28 July**
  Austria-Hungary declares war on Serbia

- **31 July**
  Russia mobilizes

- **1 August**
  Germany declares war on Russia

- **3 August**
  Germany declares war on France

- **4 August**
  Britain declares war on Germany

- **23 August**
  Japan enters the war

- **1 November**
  Russia declares war on Turkey

- **23 May**
  Italy enters the war

- **24 April**
  Irish nationalist rebellion in Dubl[in]

The Western Front

- **2 August**
  Germany invades Belgium

- **7 August**
  The Germans take Liège

- **20 August**
  The Germans take Brussels

- **21 August**
  The British Expeditionary Force arrives in France

- **23 August**
  ✕ Mons

- **26 August**
  ✕ Le Cateau

- **1 September**
  ✕ Néry

- **6–10 September**
  ✕ The Marne

1914–1915
Wet winter

20 December 1914 to 17 March 1915
✕ Champagne

10–13 March
✕ Neuve-Chapelle

- **22 April**
  First use by Germany of chlorine gas

- **May**
  Fokker adapts the machine gun for use in an airplane

25 September–8 October
✕ Loos

- **19 December**
  First use by Germans of phosgene gas
  mixed with chlorine gas

21 February–18 December
✕ Verdun

1 July–18 November
✕ The Somme

- **15 Sept[ember]**
  First us[e]

The Wider War

- **20 August**
  ✕ Gumbinnen

23–31 August
✕ Tannenberg

- **26 August**
  The Allies capture Togoland

- **30 August**
  The Allies capture Samoa

- **11 October**
  Russia attacks the German army in Poland

- **16 December**
  The German navy shells towns
  on Britain's east coast

- **19 January**
  First German airship raid on England

- **25 April**
  Gallipoli landings

- **7 May**
  Lusitania sunk

- **6 August**
  Suvla Bay landings at Gallipoli

- **1 September**
  Czar Nicholas
  takes control
  of Russian troops

- **31 May**
  ✕ Jutland

4 June–20 September
Brusilov offensive

- **2 Septemb[er]**
  First zepp[elin]
  over Brita[in]

1914   1915   1916